The Narrow Gate

32 Insights into Understanding His Word

By Fran Heron

The Narrow Gate

Copyright © 2019 Fran Heron

All rights reserved.

Unless otherwise indicated, all Scripture quotations are taken from the New King James Version. Copywrite 1982 by Thomas Nelson, Inc.

Scripture quotations marked (AMP) are taken from the Amplified Bible, Copywrite 2015 by the Lockman Foundation.

Deeper Life Press

Dedication

I DEDICATE THIS BOOK TO THOSE SEEKING AFTER GOD'S HEART, ESPECIALLY THOSE WHO HAVE RECENTLY DEDICATED THEIR LIVES TO JESUS CHRIST. MAY HE TAKE YOU ON THE GREATEST JOURNEY OF YOUR LIFE! BE ASSURED YOU WILL FIND OTHERS ON THE SAME PATH AS YOU THAT WILL ENCOURAGE YOU ALONG THE WAY!

Acknowledgements

Many thanks to my good friends Paul and Sharon Grubner. You both have encouraged me to press forward in writing this book. You would not let me give up because you thought I had something to say that would benefit others in their journey of faith.

I also need to acknowledge Adrienne Evans of AF Ministries, who once made a statement saying, "I want to see a copy of that the next time I see you." As an evangelist, life coach and trainer, I have benefited from her insight enormously!

Without the inspiration of the Holy Spirit, this would not be possible.

With Him all things are possible!

TABLE OF CONTENTS

Dedication.. iii

Acknowledgements...iv

Introduction...viii

Part 1

Chapter 1: Understanding Faith.......................................2

Chapter 2: The Narrow Gate 4

Chapter 3: An Invitation...6

Chapter 4: The Godly Kind Of Relationship 8

Chapter 5: Ask 10

Chapter 6: Knock 11

Chapter 7: Seek...12

Chapter 8: A Great Treasure 13

TABLE OF CONTENTS

Chapter 9: What Is Your Mountain?............................ 15

Chapter 10: How To Get Faith 17

Chapter 11: Prayer - The Connection 19

Chapter 12: Be Free 21

Chapter 13: Comparison 22

Chapter 14: Truth 23

Chapter 15: Take A Hold Of Your Blessings 25

Chapter 16: The Beatitudes 27

Chapter 17: Astounding Thought 29

Chapter 18: Humility 31

Chapter 19: God Forgives 33

Chapter 20: Not By Works 35

Chapter 21: His Strength 37

Chapter 22: Only Believe 39

Chapter 23: Thankfulness 41

Chapter 24: Stillness 43

Chapter 25: The Greatest Commandment 45

Chapter 26: Do Not Worry 47

Chapter 27: The Living Word 49

Chapter 28: The Unseen 51

Chapter 29: God's Faithfulness 53

Chapter 30: God's Eye 55

Chapter 31: The Resurrection 57

Chapter 32: The Armor Of God 60

Part 2

A New Day 64

Your Extravagance 65

Favor 66

Peace 67

Healing 68

Provision 69

Patience 70

Wisdom 71

Protection 72

TABLE OF CONTENTS

Hope 73

Courage 74

Love 75

Salvation 76

About The Author 77

Introduction

Just maybe you were searching for a book about how to understand God. Who is He? Does He indeed relate to me in some fashion? It is my hope that this book, one of many you may come across, will clarify some questions you might have that need answering.

The most comprehensive place to search is the Holy Bible. It is tangible and visible. You can hold it in your hands. It has been proven to be the most read book throughout the ages. Many versions are on the market, which makes it easy to understand the meaning of some passages that might need more illumination or explaining.

God also reveals Himself to us in another way. He speaks to us by means of the Holy Spirit directly to our hearts, when we pray.

It's my desire to help you, the reader, understand more about God's Son, Jesus Christ, and the Holy Spirit. As you can imagine, since I am the writer, it is experiential. It comes from my perspective. Then it will become your

Introduction

perspective as He teaches you. I have experienced Him both ways—through the written Word of God, the Bible, and through the Holy Spirit as He speaks to my heart when I pray.

Both ways give me a clear understanding of His divine character. I'm always learning as well as seeking a closer relationship with our Creator. He created us with a purpose in mind. The Bible tells us to ask, to seek, and to knock. It's time to begin your personal relationship with Him. It's an exciting journey! Your Bible will be an excellent source in understanding who God is!

PART 1

CHAPTER 1

UNDERSTANDING FAITH

You and I possess faith in everyday things without our conscious awareness! When you are at a stop light, you engage your faith. You assume that the traffic will flow accordingly. When you make an appointment at your physician's office, you assume that he will meet your expectations. When you work a 40-hour work week, you have faith that the check will be issued to you at the end of the week. These are just a few simple examples of how our faith comes into play.

In the same way our faith is activated in the spiritual sense. We don't always see in the natural sense what we are praying for. We bring our requests before God with the faith we possess at that moment. Then we remain optimistic that God will indeed hear and answer us.

The scripture says, **"For we walk by faith and not by sight"** (2 Corinthians 5:7).

You may not see with your physical eyes that your paycheck is being processed, but by faith you expect it. You may not see that the traffic is always following the laws accordingly, but by faith you expect it to flow that way. You may not see the doctor preparing to see you, but you expect him to keep the appointment.

With God, since He is a spirit, we most likely do not see Him. But we walk by faith and not by sight as the Scripture encourages us. We have the assurance and confidence that He will respond to our prayers. That could take a big leap of faith on your part, and it may seem unnatural.

But the more you walk by faith, the easier it will become and you will soon see the manifestations being worked out on your behalf. Give it some time to develop and don't get discouraged along the way! Faith will indeed come!

CHAPTER 2

THE NARROW GATE

Jesus told his disciples to enter by the narrow gate. He says there are few who find it. But it is not for a select group that would leave some out. It is for whoever desires to come into relationship with Him!

He never forces Himself on anyone. It is a choice with no strings attached. And yet it is a commitment to lead a life in harmony with Him and His kingdom principles.

He goes on to teach that many go in by the wide gate. This one would lead to a life of destruction. Let us hear how He describes it:

"Enter by the narrow gate: for wide is the gate and broad is the way that leads to destruction, and there are many who go in by it. Because narrow is the gate and difficult is the way which leads to life, and there are few who find it" (Matthew 7:13).

The Narrow Gate

Here we see two paths to choose between. Through the wide gate or the narrow gate. Think about the one you desire to enter, not a difficult choice when you see who is on the other side.

John 10:9 speaking of Jesus says, "I am the door. If anyone enters by Me, He will be saved, and will go in and out and find pasture." Jesus is the Good Shepherd who lays down his life for His sheep.

Both passages explain it all. We enter by the narrow gate and go through the door who is Jesus. That is good news, believe it!

CHAPTER 3

AN INVITATION

I am sure at some sporting event you have seen a sign held up with a popular scripture on it—John 3:16 in bold letters. It goes as follows:

"For God so loved the world that He gave His only begotten Son that whoever believes in Him should not perish but have everlasting life."

Consider yourself a whoever, for you are one! Here in this verse Jesus explained to a man named Nicodemus about salvation. He told him that in order to enter the kingdom of God one must be born again.

"How does one do that?" you might ask. There is a way and I will lay this out for you. By asking Jesus into your life there is a transition from one kingdom into another. From the kingdom of darkness to the kingdom of light. It is a prayer that must come from your heart and a willingness to change to a lifestyle totally different from the one you are presently living.

It can go something like this: "Jesus, I believe you went to the cross not only for my own sins but for those of the whole world. I turn away from my sins right now. I am sorry for them. Forgive me now. Come into my life and make me whole. I ask you to be Lord of my life and to guide me by your Spirit. Help me to walk in newness of life. Thank you, Jesus!"

If you responded to the invitation, you are born of the Spirit.

CHAPTER 4

THE GODLY KIND OF RELATIONSHIP

When we came into this world, we were born with a sin nature. There was a chasm that we inherited because of Adam's sin. There was a distance between heaven and Earth. The Bible tells us that all of us have sinned. None of us is perfect. In one way or another we have transgressed the laws and guidelines put into place that would keep us from committing misdeeds or wrongdoing.

It is sad to say, but crime is rampant in society. Our prisons are filled to overflowing, a result of that sin nature I just mentioned. Most of us are familiar with the Ten Commandments given to Moses. Breaking even one of those is a transgression against God or our fellow neighbor.

But the good news is we don't have to condemn ourselves. Don't get me wrong, sin has consequences. But there is a better way. We can make choices to turn things around. Keep reading!

The gift of God is eternal life. We don't have to beg, borrow or steal to get a life free from sin. It is ours for the asking. God is always in the business of restoring a relationship with His creation!

"The wages of sin is death, but the gift of God is eternal life in Christ Jesus Our Lord." You can read this in Romans 6:23. This is speaking of the price of sin leading to spiritual death, or an eternity without God.

The price of salvation has already been bought and paid for through the sacrifice of Jesus on the cross. We don't have to live without our Redeemer in eternity when we accept the price He paid for us.

Perhaps this all sounds new to you, a relationship with the living God. But it is a glorious one!

CHAPTER 5

ASK

The Gospel of John is perhaps a good way to dive into the Bible or, in other words, God's Word to us. Here we see how our salvation came about in the Person of Jesus Christ. Man was separated from God when sin came into the world through Adam.

Through John's writings we see restoration and redemption take place in the life, death and resurrection of Jesus Christ. God sent His only Son to Earth because He so loved the world! He has always loved us before time began, after man sinned and now as we walk in the newness of life. God has restored us so we can have fellowship with Him.

It is a journey we can all take, and it begins by asking God to share His life with us. If you want to get to know Him, take the first step by just asking Him to make Himself known to you. He will! He does not turn away anyone with a sincere heart.

CHAPTER 6

KNOCK

Jesus tells us to knock and it will be open to us in Matthew 7 verse 7.

Then, in the Book of Revelation, the last book of the Bible, He confirms this: "Behold I stand at the door and knock."

If we are willing, we can do just that—knock! He is on the other side and will open the door for us. This is not a one-time event either. Every time we knock, He will open the door to us. That is a guarantee.

Isn't it wonderful to know that God does not have favorites! He will not refuse anyone who knocks at His door. Your age, your race, or your religion does not disqualify you for any reason. He always holds out the welcome mat, any day, anytime, anywhere. No standing in lines, no waiting until He is not busy or for us to clean up our act. We come as we are with no pretense or any fancy words. He is waiting for us to come as we are.

Reference: 3:20 "Behold I stand at the door and knock. If anyone hears my voice and opens the door, I will come into him and dine with him, and he with Me."

CHAPTER 7

SEEK

Read Matthew 6:33. It challenges us in the following way: **"But seek first the kingdom of God and His righteousness, and all these things shall be added to you."**

Seeking God should become our top priority if we want to enter the most glorious relationship offered to us. It will require searching for Him with no agenda but to explore who God is to us on a personal level.

God made us in His image. Read that again! That is a powerful statement! Look in the mirror and smile when you say that. I don't know about you, but I could meditate on that all day long and will never realize its full impact on me. It makes me want to seek Him more and I hope it does the same with you. You are made in His image!

CHAPTER 8

A GREAT TREASURE

Think for a moment about the things you treasure in life. Your family, your friends, your home, your community, your job, your vacation if you are planning one, to name a few.

Yet there is one more significant thing to bring to your attention. That is the Word of God, also called the Bible. Psalm 119 is a very long psalm; in fact, it contains 176 verses! The ones I want to reference here are verses 161-162:

"But my heart stands in awe of your word. I rejoice at your word as one who finds a great treasure."

We know that the physical things in this life are temporary. One day, when we leave this earth and reach our eternal destination, the material things we have cherished in life will be left behind. In fact, the material things we have cherished, all our possessions, have a shelf life and will decay. A sobering thought, isn't it?

A GREAT TREASURE

Speaking of treasures, Jesus tells us a good rule of thumb regarding our earthly treasures: It is found in Matthew 6:19-21.

"Do not lay up for yourselves treasures on earth, where moth and rust destroy and where thieves break in and steal; but lay up for yourselves treasures in heaven, where neither moth nor rust destroys and where thieves do not break in and steal. For where your treasure is, there your heart will be also."

These verses are good for spiritual housecleaning!

CHAPTER 9

WHAT IS YOUR MOUNTAIN?

In nature we think of a mountain as a massive amount of land that is at a great height. In our spiritual walk it can mean something that is in our way preventing us from obtaining a desired result.

It may be a mountain of debt, a mountain of sickness, an obstruction that prevents us from fulfilling God's plan, or any appearance of an impossibility. I am sure you can add to this list! You begin to wonder how you can move this mountain or even get over it. You don't want to let it get the best of you, that is for sure.

Turn to Matthew 17:20 in your Bible. I hope you have one by now. Jesus, speaking to His disciples, says the following:

"..if you have faith as a mustard seed, you will say to this mountain move from here to there, and it will move; and nothing will be impossible for you."

WHAT IS YOUR MOUNTAIN?

A mustard seed is known to be a very small seed. Your faith might seem small at this time. But that doesn't matter. You and I can take this small seed and move the mountain that is obstructing our path.

God has dealt to each of us a measure of faith (Romans 12:3). What will you do with the measure He has given you? Will that mountain keep obstructing your view? Or will you begin chipping away at it until it becomes a little molehill? Use your mustard seed faith!

CHAPTER 10

HOW TO GET FAITH

Faith when used as a noun means to put trust or confidence in. It is not always used in the spiritual sense as we well know. For example, we have faith in the law of gravity. If you were to jump off a tall building, no two ways about it, you would smash into the ground below!

When we activate our faith in God, we trust that what we are believing for will surely come to pass. Romans 10:17 explains how we can acquire our faith. It goes like this:

"So then, faith comes by hearing, and hearing by the word of God." Let me explain what this means. Every time we open the Bible and read it, especially out loud, our faith grows!

An easy way to accomplish this so that it will not seem like an enormous task is to invest in a daily Bible reading. This will get you acquainted with both the Old and

HOW TO GET FAITH

New Testament. Soon you will see for yourself that your faith will grow. The important thing is to stick with it! Find a translation that will be easy for you to understand.

CHAPTER 11

PRAYER - THE CONNECTION

Many people try to complicate prayer. They think they need to follow a format for it to be effective. Granted there are written prayers that are helpful in meeting the need to express just the right thing. We have all encountered those times when we don't know how to pray as we should.

In fact, the followers of Jesus even asked Him to teach them how to pray. He told them to acknowledge their Father in heaven and to praise Him. His desire was to see the Father's kingdom come and His will to be done here on this earth. He talked about God's provision and forgiving others. Furthermore, He showed them the necessity to pray so that they would not fall into temptation and to be delivered from evil. He gave these guidelines to teach them how to pray. This is known as the Lord's Prayer to many of us. It is found in Matthew 6:9-13.

Books upon books have been written about prayer. So how should you pray? There are many ways because, when it comes down to it, everyone must discover for himself the best way to pray. Some kneel, some lift hands in praise, some silently reflect on God, some just look up to the heavens and declare His goodness. These are only a few ways to connect with God. It is not a one size fits all to encounter God. Perhaps we can add to that list one more thing—that prayer is simply talking to God in your own words.

CHAPTER 12

BE FREE

I have discovered that I can be unrestricted in my approach to God. The good news is that He never turns us away! On the contrary, any feelings of not being worthy to call upon such a holy God quickly vanish.

There is a promise laid out in Hebrews 13:5 of the New Testament. There it clearly says, "I will never leave you nor forsake you." If you have any doubts, be assured He will not reject or abandon you. There is not one excuse that can prevent us from approaching God. No sin, no feelings of guilt, no inadequacies can prevent us from drawing near to God.

I hope this takes a big weight off your shoulder. One you were not meant to carry. Be assured God will always welcome you. He longs to hear what you have to say.

Enjoy the freedom. He has already put out the welcome mat for you!

Remember, He will never leave you nor forsake you, that is His promise to you.

CHAPTER 13

COMPARISON

As human beings we have the tendency to compare ourselves to others, especially those we think have a stronger relationship with God. We shrink back, thinking we can never measure up to their standards.

The good news is that it doesn't matter one iota! God does not have favorites. He loves each of us and values each of us the same. When Jesus went willingly to the cross, He had all of us in mind. There was enough love to go around for you and me.

John 3:17 tells us that God did not send His Son into the world to condemn the world but that the world through Him might be saved. When we compare ourselves to others, I believe we diminish His great sacrifice. Jesus accepts us enough to go to the cross for each of us individually! That is the Gospel message, the Gospel of truth!

CHAPTER 14

TRUTH

How often have we heard the words, "Tell me the truth"? Perhaps you have said it to your child, or heard it in a court of law, or a teacher has confronted a student with these very words. We expect to get a truthful answer back. If we don't, be assured there will be consequences!

When Jesus was brought to Pilate's court before His crucifixion, this is the question He was asked of Him: "What is truth?" Little did Pilate realize that Jesus was the truth personified! The truth the Bible speaks of was standing right in front of him!

John 14:6 declares, "I am the Way, the Truth and the Life."

In our busy day-to-day life many are searching and asking the same question. What is truth? We too have the answer right in front of us!

TRUTH

As we open the Bible, we connect to the truth. The Gospel writers—Matthew, Mark, Luke and John—who walked with Jesus give us a clear understanding of the meaning of truth.

CHAPTER 15

TAKE A HOLD OF YOUR BLESSINGS

Psalm 112:1 begins with this verse: **"Blessed is the man who fears the Lord, who delights in His commandments."** There is no gender implied here by any means. It is referring to both man and woman. That leaves no one out.

The word fear here does not denote anything frightening either. Rather what it is referring to is being reverent in our worship towards God.

Now, getting into what blessings can be obtained. This fortunate person conducts his affairs with discretion (verse 5). His offspring will be mighty (verse 2). He will be prosperous (verse 3)! He gives to the poor (verse 9). He won't be afraid of evil tidings because he trusts in the Lord (verse 7).

Deuteronomy 28 also expounds on the blessings to the one who keeps God's commandments. In fact, the blessings will overtake you!

It says you will be blessed in the city and in the field (verse 3). God will defeat your enemies (verse 7). Your basket and your kneading bowl will be blessed (verse 5). You shall have a surplus of goods too (verse 11). Therefore, you can give to the needy.

These blessings are here for all of us. Our part as believers is to become acquainted with God's ways. Once we do that and adhere to His commandments, these blessings will overtake us.

CHAPTER 16

THE BEATITUDES

Jesus did many teachings in his ministry here on Earth, one of which was His discourse on a mountain. As you might already know, it is referred to as the Beatitudes. There were no sound systems back then, but the crowds did indeed hear him!

You can look up the full discourse in Matthew's Gospel.

He declares many who are blessed, and this encompasses many of us in our journey of faith. Perhaps you have encountered some of these emotions at one time or another in your life.

He says those who are humble or poor in spirit will have the kingdom of heaven. Comfort will come to those who mourn. The meek will inherit the earth. Those who hunger for righteousness will be satisfied. The merciful will have mercy extended to them. Those who are pure in heart will see God! Those who make peace are called the sons of God. Those who are persecuted according to righteousness will be rewarded in heaven.

Have you discovered that you found yourself in any of these situations? It certainly can give us hope in our journey of faith!

CHAPTER 17

ASTOUNDING THOUGHT

Psalm 139 has some incredible thoughts to meditate on! An amazing concept is found in verse 16. It may stretch your imagination and your faith! Before your existence, the days of your life were recorded in God's book! He goes on to say in the following verse, "How precious also are Your thoughts to me, O God! How great is the sum of them!"

That tells me that God knew us before we set foot on this planet! Not only that but that this great loving God of this universe thinks about us a great deal!

Verse 3 of this most excellent psalm goes as follows: "You comprehend my path and my lying down and are acquainted with all my ways." Seems incredible, doesn't it? Indeed, God must know us better than we know ourselves.

Verse 7 asks us a profound question. The psalmist declares, "Where can I flee from Your presence?" You see,

ASTOUNDING THOUGHT

He is always there. He doesn't ever abandon us. Even when we don't feel Him near, He still has us in mind. Remember, how great is the sum of His thoughts towards us! So ask yourself the question, and I dare say there is no place hidden where God will not be ever present to you!

CHAPTER 18

HUMILITY

What does it mean to be humble? It basically denotes not thinking of yourself more highly than others. It often involves taking the lower position.

Take a look at a prophet in the Old Testament named Micah. He is probably a prophet that most are unfamiliar with. At any rate he mentions walking in humility in the following verse:

"**He has shown you, O man, what is good; and what the Lord requires of you but to do justly, to love mercy, and to walk humbly with your God**" (Micah 6:8).

Jesus, of course, is our best example of one who walked humbly. He was God yet came in the likeness of man. Philippians 2: 8 tells us, "**And being found in appearance of man, He humbled himself and became obedient to the point of death.**"

The disciples of Jesus point blank asked Him who was the greatest in His kingdom. He assured them that whoever humbles themselves like a little child, that one is the greatest (Matthew 18:4).

James 4:6 reminds us that God resists the proud but gives grace to the humble. Further on in that same chapter James tells us, "**Humble yourself in the sight of the Lord and He will lift you up**" (James 4:10).

Some would look at being humble in a negative way. Not so; in fact, look at the second part of this scripture: "**For whoever exalts himself will be humbled, and he who humbles himself will be exalted**" (Luke 14:11). Here we see the importance of taking the low place.

CHAPTER 19

GOD FORGIVES

How many times have each of us felt sorry because we have done the wrong thing or said the wrong thing? At one time or another we have all done someone wrong or offended another intentionally or without realizing it. Or, looking at it another way, someone has offended us.

Mistakes happen. We all need forgiveness for the healing of our souls. If we don't seek forgiveness, we bury it deep. That certainly doesn't help matters. The inner turmoil can quickly change into bitterness. It is hard to like a bitter person.

Let's see some things God says about forgiveness. Psalm 103:3 referring to God says, "Who forgives all your iniquities." That word iniquity means a great injustice. If we have offended another, God offers forgiveness for the offence. And we too can extend forgiveness to the one who has injured us. Sometimes that takes a lot of courage.

GOD FORGIVES

One of Jesus' disciples, named Peter, asked Him how many times it is necessary to forgive those who sin against us. To his amazement, Jesus tells him seventy times seven! You can read that for yourself in Matthew 18:22. That is a lot of times; let's hope it gets easier the more we do it!

Mark 11:26 also gives us insight into forgiveness. Jesus says, "But if you do not forgive, neither will your Father in heaven forgive you your trespasses." That clears up a lot of gray area in our thinking.

In John 8:4 we read about a woman caught in adultery, which meant, according to the laws in the Old Testament, her punishment would be stoning! Legalistic men were trying to trap Jesus. But He did not allow that. Instead He forgave her, a life-changing moment indeed for her!

God is always offering forgiveness, let us take the higher road and do the same! It is good for the soul!

CHAPTER 20

NOT BY WORKS

There is a clarification in the Book of Ephesians about how we get saved. Some think that it is by our own efforts that we earn our way into a saving relationship with Jesus Christ. Not so.

Look at Ephesians 2:8 to see what I mean. "For by grace you have been saved through faith, and that not of yourselves; it is the gift of God, not of works, lest anyone should boast."

Sometimes we are so busy concentrating on our own good deeds that we leave God out of the picture. A non-believer thinks he can earn his way to heaven. They surmise these good works are enough to merit heaven.

The reality is God extends His loving kindness to us with no strings attached. It is His grace that enables us to be born again into His kingdom. He does not take into consideration our worthiness. Truthfully none of us could possibly qualify. There are no point systems in His kingdom. That leaves no room for us to brag in a prideful way. Any good deeds we do are out of our love for Him and the people we encounter in our daily lives.

In conclusion, it is God's grace and mercy that allows us to be partakers of salvation in Christ. No merit badges on our part. No works to earn the way of salvation.

CHAPTER 21

HIS STRENGTH

When we need strength, when we need to be empowered, it is essential for us to look to God. It says it well in Philippians 4:13:

"I can do all things through Christ who strengthens me." That scripture alone gives me the needed assurance that whatever circumstances I am in at the time, I can go to Christ and He will intervene. He will give me the ability to overcome and the courage to press on and not give up in seemingly impossible situations.

In Psalm 19 verse 14 the Lord is literally called **"my strength**". Another way to put it is that He is our Rock. All of us at times feel weak with little or no strength to make it on our own.

As we call out to God, He promises us this in Psalm 18:32: "It is God who arms me with strength and makes my way perfect." It is almost like He wields His weapons in our battles. He guides us and helps us overcome our struggles.

Jesus was once asked, "**What is the greatest commandment?**" **He responded, "And you shall love the Lord your God with all your heart, with all your soul, with all your mind, and with all your strength**" (Mark 12:30).

As we adhere to that commandment, as we exchange our strength for His, we are on our way to living victoriously!

CHAPTER 22

ONLY BELIEVE

A common word in our English language is believe. We use it frequently, if not all the time. I am sure you have said, "I believe so."

It involves your understanding something to be true. It is an acceptance of the facts to be correct. Sometimes we have underlying doubts about the matter but are willing to agree with the premises.

In Mark's Gospel, chapter 5:36, Jesus tells a man named Jairus, "Do not be afraid; only believe." He had a daughter who was close to dying. He saw Jesus and literally begged Him to heal her.

Jesus was willing to do this, and on His way to Jairus's house, He met another person who had need of healing. Jesus was well known as a healer and people crowded around Him. It was His mission now to heal this woman!

ONLY BELIEVE

Now, the friends of Jairus thought it was too late for healing to take place for his daughter. Time had passed and Jesus came with some of his disciples to the house of Jairus. The girl had no life in her.

Perhaps Jairus was pondering what Jesus had told him earlier. He told him to ONLY BELIEVE. Imagine what he was thinking then when he saw his twelve-year-old daughter lying on her deathbed. Perhaps he had a lot of unbelief to counteract. We might be the same too in this situation.

But Jesus knew that He would raise this girl and bring her back to life. As the story goes, He did just that, restored her to her family. As you can rightly imagine, they were amazed and once again had reason to rejoice.

Sometimes we find ourselves in impossible situations, perhaps not as serious as the one Jairus experienced. Our faith may not seem enough to overcome obstacles. We try in our own strength to believe we can, but it is often not enough. But like Jairus in this Gospel of Mark, we need to call upon Jesus because He is willing to come to our aid.

His promise still rings true throughout the ages. **ONLY BELIEVE**! It's true for us today. Put your faith in Him.

CHAPTER 23

THANKFULNESS

Thankfulness is such a pleasant word. It denotes our gratitude and appreciation for someone or something we are pleased with. When a person shows his appreciation by just saying thanks, it does our heart good.

Psalm 95:2 reads, "**Let us come before Him with thanksgiving; let us shout joyfully to Him with psalms.**" We see here that when we pray, it is important to acknowledge God in the spirit of thanksgiving. A thankful heart always produces good results. It opens the door of fellowship to the one who created us.

Another verse along these same lines is: Psalm 100:4, which encourages us as follows: "**Enter into His gates with thanksgiving, and into His courts with praise.**" As we do this, we have His attention.

Think of your own spouse or your children. Whenever they express gratitude, it encourages us to bless them even more. We know that they appreciate what we do for them, especially when it is a heartfelt "Thank you!"

When Jesus shared His last Passover meal, which we call the Last Supper, with his disciples, He gave thanks to His Father in Heaven for the bread and the fruit of the vine (the cup). He knew the importance of giving thanks to His Father in Heaven. He becomes our example to give thanks in all things.

Think about who you can thank today. Is it your spouse, your children, your teacher, your employer, your staff, the teller at the bank, your contractor, your brother, your sister, your friend, your waiter or waitress? The list goes on and on, it's endless. Try not to leave anyone out, especially our Lord and Savior Jesus Christ!

CHAPTER 24

STILLNESS

In our fast-paced society, stillness seems to be an uncommon trait. Social media is forever summoning us to check our phones, Facebook, our text messages, Instagram, check out the latest YouTube songs or whatever media you choose.

Seems almost impossible to tune things out if it were not for turning off the lights and calling it a night. Even then it is difficult to quiet ourselves since the events of the day are still uppermost in our thoughts.

God challenges us in these eight words: "**Be still and know that I am God**" (Psalm 46:10). Isn't it refreshing to know that there is someone in control of the universe and our lives as well? We can remain tranquil when the clatter tries to usurp our peace. Serenity can be maintained when we reflect on the awesomeness that indeed He is God.

STILLNESS

Many know and have recited the twenty-third psalm. It starts out, "The Lord is my shepherd." I'm sure you know the one I am referring to. Verse 2 reads, "He leads me beside the still waters." Often it seems like our thoughts are drowning in violent waters. In Mark's Gospel Jesus was with his disciples in a boat and a storm ensued. They were fearful but Jesus took command and said, "**Peace, be still!**" (Mark 4:39). The storm ceased and much to their surprise their calmness was restored.

Here we see an example of how we can invite Jesus into our boat when we feel overwhelmed and peace seems far from us. He is the anchor of our soul and will calm our restlessness.

CHAPTER 25

THE GREATEST COMMANDMENT

Both the Old Testament and the New Testament give us the same directive to live an exemplary life. This model stated in the Book of Deuteronomy is repeated in the Gospels of the New Testament. This leaves no confusion or doubt as they complement each other.

The writer in Deuteronomy 6:4-5 states the following: "Hear O Israel: The Lord our God, the Lord is one! You shall love the Lord your God with all your heart, with all your soul, and with all your strength." This commandment was to be taught to their children thereby lengthening their days on this earth and ensuring that all would go well with them.

In the New Testament recorded in Matthew 22:37 we read about a lawyer trying to test Jesus. He questioned Him as to what the greatest commandment is. Jesus studied the scriptures and knew what was written in the law. He was always amazing his listeners. His response was the following:

"You shall love the Lord your God with all your heart, with all your soul, and with all your mind." This is the first and the greatest commandment. And the second is like it. "You shall love your neighbor as yourself. On these two commandments hang all the Law and the Prophets." Mark's Gospel further tells us that the man questioning him replies that Jesus has spoken the truth.

In our walk with the Lord, wherever He takes us in our journey, these commandments serve to be models for us to live a strong Christian life.

CHAPTER 26

DO NOT WORRY

Does the title on this page make you question even the remotest possibility of not worrying?

There is a scripture passage that instructs us to do just that. Jesus taught about it, and we would do well to heed His words. He knows our human nature and how we are prone to ruminate. We constantly worry about our children, our debts, our future, our grades, our employment, our friendships, any predicament that comes our way. I am sure you can add to this short list.

The reference I am referring to here is in Matthew the sixth chapter. It begins with verse 25: "Therefore I say to you, do not worry about your life, what you will eat or what you will drink; nor about your body, what you will put on. Is not life more than food and the body more than clothing?"

Then, in verse 27, He asks a question: "Which of you by worrying can add one cubit to his stature?" Certainly,

DO NOT WORRY

we cannot grow an inch in height by worrying. This may sound silly, but it's true indeed.

Further on down in that passage He tells us that Our heavenly Father knows all our needs. For us to have our needs met, He gives us the solution. "**But seek first the kingdom of God and Hs righteousness all these things shall be added to you**" (Matthew 6:33).

I counted five times in this passage in Matthew where Jesus commands us not to worry. Let's begin to take Him at His word.

There is one more verse that Jesus presents to us and is practical:

Verse 34 of that passage reads, "Therefore do not worry about tomorrow, for tomorrow will worry about its own things. Sufficient for the day is its own trouble."

CHAPTER 27

THE LIVING WORD

Before Jesus became manifested in the flesh, God spoke to man by other means. He did this by means of His prophets. Perhaps you have heard of some of them. Isaiah, Jeremiah, and Ezekiel are some of the familiar ones. Hosea, Amos and Obadiah are ones you may not be familiar with.

These prophets were on the scene to deliver the Word of the Lord to God's chosen ones, the people of Israel. They were being prepared as a nation to usher in the birth of the Messiah. They foretold of a Savior who would rule in righteousness and holiness.

John the Baptist was the immediate forerunner who preceded Jesus' ministry. He was the voice of one crying in the wilderness to prepare the way of the Lord (Luke 3:4, Matt 3:3, Mark 1:3, John 1:23). John preached a baptism of repentance. Then the greater one, Jesus, the Messiah, was baptized by John and so began His personal ministry.

THE LIVING WORD

Jesus was the eternal Word from the beginning of time. John 1:1 declares, "In the beginning was the Word, and the Word was with God, and the Word was God."

We see that in the fullness of time, as recorded in John 1:14, the following: "And the Word became flesh and dwelt among us, and we beheld His glory, the glory of the only begotten of the Father, full of grace and truth."

As we read the Holy Scriptures, both the Old and New Testament, we must be mindful that not only do they speak of Our Lord, but He indeed is the Living Word.

The Enduring Word lives and abides forever (1 Peter 1:23).

CHAPTER 28

THE UNSEEN

One thing about faith that we need to grasp is found in Hebrews 11 verse 1. At times what we are believing for seems way out of our reach. We wonder how we can possibly apprehend what is in the spiritual not yet revealed in the natural.

Paul the Apostle, writer of the Book of Hebrews, says this: "Now faith is the substance of things hoped for, the evidence of things not seen." Even more astounding is the tense used here. "Now." Not some time in the future but this present time. God is eternal and is not confined to time like we humans are.

Let us look at another translation that will clarify this verse in Hebrews and perhaps make it less difficult for us to lay hold of. This reference is indeed easier to absorb. It is from the Amplified Version of the Bible.

"Now faith is the assurance (the confirmation, the title deed) of things [we] hope for, being the proof of things

[we] do not see and the conviction of their reality [faith perceiving as real fact what is not revealed to the senses]."

This indicates to me that faith being a substance, and faith being an assurance, and faith having the proof all bring it down to the natural. Just as a title deed gives you proof of ownership, so faith becomes the title deed to what you are believing for the moment you activate your faith.

Another verse I would like to cross reference here expresses the importance of seeing the invisible... "**while we do not look at the things which are seen, but the things which are not seen. For the things which are seen are temporary, but the things which are not seen are eternal**" (2 Corinthians 4:18).

The more we use our faith, the more the intangible becomes tangible!

CHAPTER 29

GOD'S FAITHFULNESS

Who is faithful? You may answer that by saying, "My husband, my children, my paperboy, the person who plows me out in the winter storms, my hairdresser who cuts my hair just the way I like it, my auto repair guy that I can depend on not to overcharge me, my dog who greets me after a hard day at the office." These are just a few of many that we take for granted.

Have you ever included God in this category of faithfulness? We can depend on Him for He is trustworthy and dependable. He is committed to you and I can honestly say devoted to you. He is a loyal companion to those who put their trust in Him.

Psalm 119:90 says this about God: "**Your faithfulness endures to all generations.**" It wasn't just for prophets of old, men and women who were spokespersons for their generation. He is equally as faithful in our generation as well.

Upon arising each day, we can be sure He is committed to us. Lamentations 3:22-23 reminds us of God's faithfulness. **"Through the Lord's mercies we are not consumed because His compassions fail not. They are new every morning; Great is your faithfulness."**

In the New Testament, we see faithfulness as one of the fruits of the Spirit. So not only is God faithful to us, but we are encouraged as well to be faithful to those in our sphere of influence.

"But the fruit of the Spirit is love, joy, peace, longsuffering, kindness, goodness, faithfulness, gentleness, self-control" (Galatians 5:22).

We would do well to deliberately reflect on God's faithfulness to us; perhaps soon we will abound in this God-given fruit of the Spirit.

CHAPTER 30

GOD'S EYE

As we know, we all were born with five senses, seeing being one of them. Have you ever thought about God's eye? I imagine if you are like me probably not recently. Well, scripture tells us much about the eyes of God. I will give you a few references. They are eye-openers for the student of His Word.

Psalm 32:8 records this: "I will instruct you and teach you in the way you should go; I will guide you with My Eye." So, we see here that the Lord will direct us—He won't let us out of His sight. His eye leads us. Surely that will give us comfort in our daily affairs.

In the epistle of Peter, we read, **"For the eyes of the Lord are on the righteous, and His ears are open to their prayers"** (1 Peter 3:12).

The Book of Proverbs has something to share with us also. Perhaps you at one time wondered if God sees the evil that is prominent in our society. Well, He does.

This will clear up any questioning in your mind. Proverbs 15:3 reads, "The eyes of the Lord are in every place, keeping watch on the evil and the good." He sees it all. Both the good and the bad. There is no escaping His eyes. He saw that person you helped yesterday and the sacrifices you made even when it wasn't convenient. He also noticed the one who made a wrong choice and violated the laws of our land.

Look at a verse from 2 Chronicles 16:9. It reads as follows: "For the eyes of the Lord run to and fro throughout the whole earth, to show Himself strong on behalf of those who heart is loyal to Him." Our loyalty to God is not overlooked in His eyes. Indeed, we will see the evidence of His strong and powerful character in our lives.

CHAPTER 31

THE RESURRECTION

In our Christian heritage, the Resurrection of Jesus from the dead is the central event that changed everything. Jesus predicted that He would suffer to the point of death and rise again three days later. What He prophesied about Himself came to pass.

In the Gospel of Mark, we read the following about Jesus: "And He began to teach them that the Son of Man must suffer many things and be rejected by the elders and chief priests and scribes, and be killed, and after three days rise again. He spoke this word openly" (Mark 8:31-32). One of His close disciples, Peter, found this news too difficult to fathom as you can imagine. But the plan of God ultimately was carried out as Jesus spoke it would.

Those who associated with Jesus and came to know Him as the One sent by God to bring salvation to all men were deeply saddened at His crucifixion. Their hopes were shattered as they believed He would free them from their enemies. But His kingdom was not of this world. His heavenly Father had a greater plan that not only included His immediate followers but us as well. It was extended to all generations.

Three days passed. All things changed. Jesus' words now came to pass. The tomb where He was laid to rest was now empty. Even the stone that had been placed in front of the tomb was rolled back. Mary Magdalene was first on the scene to witness this. Her fear of not seeing Jesus where they laid Him gripped her. But an angel of the Lord appeared before her and proclaimed that He had risen!

At first, she did not recognize her Lord. But when Jesus spoke her name, as He was standing there in her midst, she knew it was Him. As much as she desired to embrace Him, He told her that He had to ascend to His father and hers.

She was overwhelmed with excitement and ran to share the good news that Jesus had risen from the dead.

Nothing like this had ever happened. Would His disciples believe this woman? Jesus knew their hearts and did not leave them to their questionings and doubts. That very day, His disciples were witnesses of His resurrection. Jesus came to where His disciples were meeting and had these words for them: "Peace be with you" (John 20..19). He then showed them His hands and His side where they pierced Him on the cross. Now they saw for themselves what Mary had witnessed earlier that day.

To this day, Christians commemorate this awesome event. We are still in awe as was Mary and Jesus' disciples. We too declare that He is Risen, just as the angel at the tomb did when Mary first came to the realization that her Lord was still alive.

CHAPTER 32

THE ARMOR OF GOD

In the natural we would not expect those who go to war to fight our battles, going into enemy territory, to be without protection. There is a protocol that they engage in to prepare to meet the enemy. Part of that is to wear special covering for their personal protection to keep them from harm. They have strategic plans practiced repeatedly should they need to engage the enemy.

Likewise, we have an enemy that wishes to engage us as believers but on an entirely different level. This enemy is in the unseen realm. He is referred to as our adversary.

1 Peter 5:8 cautions us to be aware of the devil. **"Be sober, be vigilant; because your adversary the devil walks about like a roaring lion seeking whom he may devour."**

God does not leave us defenseless. He gives us the means to protect us from our adversary. We can rest assured that His weapons are unmatched when this enemy tries to overtake us. The roaring lion will be silenced.

The tactics we must engage in so that we are not defenseless can be found in the Book of Ephesians. The apostle Paul, who wrote this book, shares with us how we can be protected in the spiritual realm. In detail he teaches us how to put on our armor to resist the devil.

Ephesians 6:10-19 outlines the armor of God that we should put on. We should put on truth, righteousness, the shield of faith, the helmet of salvation, the gospel of peace on our feet, and take up the sword of the Spirit. With these in place we can destroy the plans of the enemy of our souls.

"For we do not wrestle against flesh and blood but against principalities, against powers, against the rulers of the darkness of this age, against spiritual hosts of wickedness in heavenly places" (Ephesians 6:12). We must pray always and be watchful.

We do not wage this spiritual battle in the flesh. 2 Corinthians 10:4 says it this way: **"For the weapons of our warfare are not carnal, but mighty in God for pulling down strongholds…"**

Just as those who defend our land are prepared for battle, we too can be prepared spiritually to resist our adversary the devil.

"Therefore, submit to God. <u>Resist</u> the devil and he will flee from you" (James 4:7).

Part 2

A NEW DAY

Dear Lord,

As I start today, I want to consider how You are mindful of me, as I am of You.

I pray that I will feel Your presence as I go about my daily activities, all the while needing assurance that You are guiding me along my path.

If I stumble along the journey, I trust You will pick me up, dust me off and encourage me to press onward.

I am confident that Your blessings will overtake me at every turn. It's Your good pleasure to see to it that I have success as sure as the sun rises!

For this I give You thanks! Amen!

YOUR EXTRAVAGANCE

Today, I am meditating on Your magnificence, Lord. You created the universe and all of creation displays Your beauty!

All I have to do is to take a moment and look at the grandeur of what lies in front of me. The trees swaying in the wind, the hummingbird taking his drink at my feeder, the white clouds being carried along the blue sky. These only scratch the surface just a few feet away.

It is my prayer that I will appreciate all of it! Give me eyes to see what I never noticed before. I am sure I am missing out on a lot, but I want to experience so much more.

Remind me to take moments in my day to behold how marvelous Your original design of creation beckons my attention! Amen

FAVOR

Heavenly Father, I pray for favor today. Mary, the mother of Our Lord Jesus Christ, was given great favor to bring the Son of the living God into our world. She was preferred above all women in her day to have that great honor.

Yet I know that Your kindness is also extended to us as well. You desire to see Your children blessed. You are a gracious Father!

At times I need a special outpouring of Your support to succeed in my undertakings. Just knowing that You always back me up and support me gives me great courage in all that life demands of me.

Thank You for being my loyal and encouraging Father! Amen

PEACE

Lord, the Bible says that You are the Prince of Peace. I need You today and every day to keep me in perfect peace.

So many things are competing for my attention as soon as I wake from my sleep. My feet hit the floor and I am already thinking of what I shall do first. Endless lists. People to call, errands to run, family needs, bills to pay to name a few.

I know if I place my trust in You, my daily activities will flow like they are supposed to. Even though there are continuous interruptions, I know You will keep me composed, not rattled as my day moves along.

Help me to focus on Your guidance so that I can continuously flow in Your peace. Be my Prince of Peace! Amen

HEALING

Lord, I know when You walked this earth, You healed so many people. You opened blind eyes, healed deaf mutes, healed a woman with blood issues, cured others with leprosy. You made the lame to walk. These are just a few of the people You desired to see made whole.

I know that Your gifts of healing are still available today. It is not easy to get through life without a time when we need to call out to You for healing.

Physicians too want to see us walk in good health. You have given them the ability to correct physical problems. Yet there are times when medicine is not always the answer. More is needed.

I pray that I will look to You as My healer in every situation. It is Your desire to bring healing even in this present age, just like in the days when You walked this earth. Amen

PROVISION

Lord, You created the universe. That is a monumental statement! I should give that a lot of thought today. Nothing is small when it comes to You. I cannot fathom with my finite mind the vastness of what You brought into existence.

I would be amiss if at first I did not come to You for what I need. In fact, it gives You great pleasure to provide for Your children. Your supply is according to Your great riches.

Therefore, today I bring my needs before You. I pray for Your abundant supply to meet my essential needs. Help me to maintain a thankful heart as I anticipate your blessings for today. Amen

PATIENCE

Lord, patience is what we all need. I need to cultivate more of that in my life. It is not easy to wait; we seem to want things right now or even yesterday.

Each day I am confronted with situations that require me to be calm, to hold my composure. I am trying my utmost not to lose control. I seem to jump ahead and make decisions without knowing all the facts.

I need Your hand upon my shoulder to steady me. I need endurance to hold back the reins, take a deep breath, and, yes, pray for patience!

Above all, thank You, Lord, for Your continuous patience with me! Amen

WISDOM

Today, Lord, I pray for wisdom. Each day I need Your help to discern what course of action I should take. The big decisions as well as those small choices are always before me.

Should I accept that new position offered to me? Which car would be the safest as well as the most economical for me? Do I take that vacation this year? Is this the mate You have chosen for me? Is this the time for that conversation I need to engage in to mend that relationship? These are only a few I thought about today, good grief!

I can possess a lot of knowledge, but if I don't use it rightly, applying wisdom, then I will not succeed.

The Bible tells us that wisdom is even better than rubies. Nothing that we would want or desire can compare to wisdom.

I need Your insight and understanding to steer the course today. I am leaning on You to help me apply the experience and knowledge You have already given me. Only then will I be decisive and confident. Amen

PROTECTION

Lord, every day I am relying on your protection. None of us know ahead of time the things we might encounter as soon as we leave the security of our homes.

The weather could change without a moment's notice, creating driving problems. Even road rage is not uncommon these days. Turbulence in air flight can scare the best of us.

My prayer is that You would keep me from trouble. Guard and defend me from unseen forces that could change the course of my life. Preserve me from all harm or injury.

May You give Your angels guardianship over my life. Amen

HOPE

Lord, many a time we have used the word hope in our conversations.

"I hope for a sunny day, I am hoping for a new job, I hope to get accepted at this college, I hope I get this promotion, I hope this guy asks me out for a date, I hope I get good test results." These just scratch the surface as we live out each day.

I want my hope to be found in You. As I read the scriptures each day, I find hope in Your Word. It encourages me to be optimistic. My expectations soar as it causes me to hope for a good outcome all the time.

Abraham, our example and father in the faith, hoped to have a son promised to him by the Lord. Even though it took years for that fulfillment, he still hoped. Eventually he received the promise when Issac was born.

Help me to have that same assurance by continuing to hope without vacillating. I know as I read Your Word hope will indeed arise! Amen.

COURAGE

Lord, I need a good dose of courage today. All of us at one time or another must confront the enemy of our soul. When we face danger or fear, we often lose our nerve or boldness to confront our adversary.

I must turn to You. Only then will I not be afraid or terrified. I know You will not fail me. You will supply the courage to face what lies before me.

It may appear that the giant in my mind will overtake me. The temptation to admit defeat is overwhelming. I won't yield to fear; instead, I will yield to You. I know You have the sword drawn to protect and shield me from all harm.

I have confidence that in You, Lord, I am secure and ready to face my giant! Amen

LOVE

Love is one of the most basic of all human needs, this we know, Lord. And we all have different ways of giving love and receiving love. You have been the best example of living a life of pure love.

Your compassion was evidenced in countless ways. You fed the hungry crowd that came to hear You by multiplying the loaves and fishes from a young boy's lunch. You caused the crippled to walk again. You opened blind eyes. You welcomed young children to be around You. You forgave sinners and did not condemn. You even raised Lazarus from the dead and restored him to his family.

The Bible tells us that the greatest gift is love. We are to love You with all our hearts and to love our neighbors as ourselves. Both commands really sum up our walk with You.

Today and every day I make it my aim to place my affection on You. I want to worship You with all that is within me. Only then will I be capable of sharing that God kind of love with others. Amen

SALVATION

Lord, I come to You today to receive salvation. It is recorded in Your word, "The Lord is my light and salvation" (Psalm 27:1).

I realize that I have gone the wrong way and have sinned against You. I come to You with a repentant heart. I ask for forgiveness, knowing You died for me; You gave Your life for me by Your death on the cross.

Romans 10:9 "...that if you confess with your mouth the Lord Jesus and believe in your heart that God has raised Him from the dead, you will be saved."

Romans 10:10 "For with the heart one believes unto righteousness, and with the mouth confession is made unto salvation."

Ephesians 2:8 "For by grace you have been saved through faith, and not of yourself; it is the gift of God, not of works, lest anyone should boast."

I accept You into my heart today, Lord. Thank You for so great a salvation!

Amen!

ABOUT THE AUTHOR

Frances first came to a deeper faith in Christ during her years at a private school at the height of the Charismatic Renewal. The Holy Spirit touched her and gave her the desire to share with others her deep faith.

Her journey of faith led her to read and study God's Word daily. Her library of books by notable biblical authors provided growth in this walk of faith.

In addition to having a career with special needs children Frances has shared about her Savior, Jesus Christ, in prison ministry. She enjoys the everyday contact with people sharing as the Spirit leads be it in airports, nursing homes or the marketplace.

Frances hopes that through planting seeds of faith, more will come to know and experience how precious it is to have a relationship with Jesus Christ. It is truly a life-changing experience!

"A presence-driven publisher making your book dream come true!"

www.deeperlifepress.com

Made in the USA
Lexington, KY
14 November 2019